CW00321416

TELLY ADDICT

Game Shows

TELLY ADDICT

Game Shows

First published in the UK in 2014

© Demand Media Limited 2014

www.demand-media.co.uk

Printed and bound in Europe

ISBN 978-1-910270-07-3

Contents

Introduction

Television game shows descended from radio game shows, the very first of which were aired at the end of the 1930s with Spelling Bee being broadcast in 1938. As television game shows began infiltrating popular culture for good during the 1950s, they quickly became a fixture of popular television.

Telly Addict: Game Shows highlights over forty well-known and loved shows that have given pleasure to British

audiences for many years, in fact some of them for decades. The variety and diversity of game shows produced over the past seventy or so years is quite staggering. From Call My Bluff, Family Fortunes and Blankety Blank to Who Wants to Be a Millionaire, A Question of Sport and Eggheads, many have become household favourites that are still watched avidly by fans.

In addition to the numerous game shows themselves, many of the men and women – some who launched their careers by presenting them – have also become renowned and distinguished figures. Stars such as Bob Monkhouse, Anneka Rice, Bruce Forsyth and Cilla Black are just some of the famous and acclaimed television personalities who have featured and become synonymous with the game shows showcased here.

3-2-1

Made by Yorkshire Television for ITV and presented by former Butlins Redcoat Ted Rogers, 3-2-1 was a very popular British game show that ran for ten years between 1978 and 1988. In retrospect the show was truly cringe worthy, but at the time it was extremely popular and also Yorkshire Television's most popular game show before they produced Countdown.

The game show was actually three shows in one. Divided into three key parts, the first was a quiz show, the second a variety show and the final third part was a game show. The overall objective of the game was to try and not get eliminated and to make it through to the final round, where by successfully unravelling a series of cryptic clues would win the contestant the star prize, or the booby prize if they got it all wrong. Later on in the series the

show adopted a weekly theme such as 'Sea cruise' or the 'Swinging Sixties'. This meant that every week the theme would run through in all aspects of the show: the stage sets, quiz questions and clues.

The first quiz part – the 1000 to 1 quiz – consisted of three couples answering a maximum of ten questions with the chance to win £1,000. Two couples survived this part with the eliminated couple being given the accrued quiz prize money, plus a ceramic model of Dusty Bin. The couples then watched the variety part of the show. The likes of Bonnie Langford, Michael Ball, Frankie Howard, the Drifters, Showaddywaddy and many more performed over the years. One of the performers then gave Ted Rogers a clue object with corresponding rhyming clues for a particular prize. The couples discarded one prize before competing for

the final round with the final elimination question. This consisted of three clues, a tie-breaker question was read out and the winning couple went on to receive two more objects to which famously impenetrable cryptic clues were attached.

And who could forget Dusty Bin who was the show's mascot and booby prize. Each week Dusty Bin would be dressed in that week's theme. The show didn't really have any memorable catchphrases, but it did have Ted Roger's iconic lightening fast finger 3-2-1 movement! This became a very important gimmick of the show,

not to mention a challenge for children and adults alike to try and master it too!

The viewing figures for 3-2-1 were always consistently high. The first series, which was in fact only produced as a summer filler, in fact attracted up to sixteen and a half million viewers. The following years of the game show never failed to pull in less than twelve million. There are very few game shows of the twenty-first century who manage to get such regular viewing ratings; nine million viewers is now regarded as a magnificent achievement.

A Question of Sport

First broadcast in 1968 regionally and then from 1970 nationally, A Question of Sport is one of Britain's longest running BBC quiz shows and it is still broadcast to this day. A total of forty-three series, totalling one thousand and forty episodes at the time of writing have so far been aired.

The show has two teams, A and B, which consist of different sports stars every week, apart from the constant resident team captains, who have obviously changed over the years. The sports stars have to answer questions about their own sports as well as others. Each team captain is joined by two different sports personalities each episode.

The format of the show consists of a variety of rounds, and it is arguably due to the variety of the show that it has stood the test of time. The picture board round is a numbered board of squares from which a contestant has to identify a sports person that is revealed. The action round is where contestants are asked questions about a montage of sporting action. What Happened Next? shows sports footage that is stopped at a key moment and the teams have to guess what happened next. The observation round is a memory test from a sporting clip shown. The mystery guest is then presented and teams have to identify who it is. The Home or Away round teams can get extra points by choosing an Away question. The captain's challenge is where the two have a contest in different feats, which is followed by the one minute round of nine questions for each team. Finally, the quick fire on the buzzer round finishes the show.

There have been many team captains over the years, including on Team A, Fred

Trueman (1976 to 1977), Bill Beaumont (1982 to 1996), John Parrot (1996 to 2002), Frankie Dettori (2002 to 2004) and Matt Dawson who has been Team A captain since 2004. Notable Team B captains have included Henry Cooper (1970 to 1979), Emlyn Hughes (1979 to 1981), Ian Botham (1988 to 1996), Ally McCoist (1996 to 2007), and current Team B captain Phil Tufnell who took over the position in 2008.

The very first series was presented by Stuart Hall and then by David Vine, British television sports presenter from 1970 to 1978. Sports commentator David Coleman then took the reins from 1979 until 1997. Former professional tennis player and television presenter Sue Barker took the position when David Coleman retired and has been presenting the programme ever since.

The format of A Question of Sport was so successful that it led to the creation of several other spin-off BBC game shows including A Question of Pop, presented by Jamie Theakston, A Question of News, presented by Richard Baker, A Question of Entertainment, presented by Tom O'Connor and A Question of TV, presented by Gaby Roslin.

Big Break

Created by Roger Medcalf, Mike Kemp and Terry Mardell, British game show Big Break was first broadcast by the BBC in 1991 and ran until 2002. Totalling fourteen series and two hundred and twenty-two episodes, including seventeen specials, the game show was a combination of traditional game show elements but based around the game of snooker.

The show was presented by comedian Jim Davidson and the former snooker player and later commentator John Virgo. The chemistry between them often created the light-hearted and comic tone that the show was renowned for. Davidson would frequently mock Virgo in some way, perhaps what he was wearing for example. Due to this banter and Davidson's constant poking at him, audiences became sympathetic to Virgo.

Virgo did, however, sometimes lash back at Davidson, which again, enhanced the light and comic tone of the show.

The show began by Davidson presenting a short monologue and then presenting Virgo, who would come on with a bag of snooker balls. The contestants were then introduced before they had to select a snooker ball from the bag. The colour of this determined which professional snooker player would be on the show.

The first round was called 'Red Hot' and began by each contestant having ten seconds given on the clock. Three questions were asked and for each correct answer another ten seconds would be added. Later in the series this changed to them starting with forty seconds with five seconds being deducted for every wrong answer; this meant that the minimum

playing time became twenty-five instead of ten seconds. Whatever time the contestant had accrued was the time they had to pot as many red balls as possible. The loser of this round would be unable to then win the show, but would continue in the next round for a consolation prize.

Every episode Virgo performed a trick shot that the losing contestant would try and replicate, therefore winning a small prize. The Pocket Money round gave the contestants a chance to win actual cash. Their snooker player played the normal snooker game and each colour ball was worth different amounts of money; ten pounds for red going up to seventy pounds for the black. The pockets were also coloured, so if that colour ball was potted in the corresponding pocket, the money was doubled for that pot. If a shot was missed the contestant was asked questions to enable play to commence again. Each contestant won the money earned for them by the snooker player and the one with the most money went onto the final round.

The final Make or Break? round was a prize winning round. With five questions and ninety seconds, each correct answer took a red ball off the table. Once answered the remaining time was given to the snooker player to clear the table. One red ball and each coloured ball won the contestant a prize. If the player potted the black this won the Mystery Star Prize, sometimes a holiday.

All contestants went home with at least a Big Break trophy and a snooker cue and the game show always ended with Davidson saying 'Say goodnight, JV', to which Virgo replied 'Goodnight JV'.

Blankety Blank

Based on the original Australian game show Blankety Blanks and the American show Match Game, the British comedy game show Blankety Blank was first broadcast on BBC One in 1979. The show ran until 1990 and comprised of seventeen series and totalled two hundred and sixty-five episodes.

Blankety Blank was first hosted by Terry Wogan and then by Les Dawson and, as well as the two contestants competing, there was also a celebrity panel of six on which the likes of Kenny Everett, Lorraine Chase and Cheryl Baker sat. The celebrities were introduced first followed by the two players, with that unforgettable theme tune blasting out at the same time. The show was later revived in 1997 when it was presented by Lily Savage (Paul O'Grady).

'Blankety Blank was very …' There were several different words that could fit into the space and the game was for the contestant to match the word with the celebrity answers who played alongside them. If the contestant's answer matched with the player then a point was given. Once all six celebrities had revealed their answer, the process was repeated by the second contestant.

If after the first round a player had matched with all six celebrities they won that game. The lowest scoring contestant then went first in the next round, but they only played with the celebrities who they hadn't matched words with in the first round. If there wasn't a winner after the second round a sudden death was played out. The players wrote down an answer to the statement and then the celebrities each gave their answers in turn. The first celebrity answer to match up with one of the contestants meant that contestant had won the sudden death.

However, no losing contestant ever went home empty-handed because they won the famous Blankety Blank chequebook and pen!

The winner of round two then went through to the Supermatch Game. A legend was revealed that consisted of a two-word phrase with one word blanked out. Prior to the show the audience had been polled as to what the missing word should be. The top three answers were then hidden on a board. The contestant then picked their favourite three celebrities to play with them and to write down what they thought the missing word was. The player could either take the advice of one of these, or choose to use their own word if different. Each of the three blanks on the board were worth different points (50, 100 and 150) and as you remember, 'more blanks meant better prizes'!

The entire game was then repeated with two new contestants. The winner of which then went head to head with the winner of the first round. Better prizes were on offer at this stage, but at the end of the day if, once the player had chosen their one celebrity to help at that stage, their answer didn't match they didn't win a prize!

Blind Date

Produced by London Weekend Television and presented by Cilla Black, Blind Date was a British dating show that ran from 1985 to 2003 totalling eighteen series and three hundred and fifty-six episodes.

The format of the show was very simple. Three single people of the same sex sat on stools one side of a screen and they were asked three questions by one person of the opposite sex on the other side, accompanied by Cilla Black of course! Each of the three then had to answer three questions, and the idea was that their answer would make the question asking contestant want to pick them to go on a date. The format would then swap so that the opposite sex were lined up on the stools to answer the questions.

'Our Graham' was the voice of Graham Skidmore who worked with Cilla Black on the show from 1985 until 2002. He was replaced for the final year by Tommy Sandhu. Graham's voice from nowhere was very distinctive and he became as much a part of the show as Cilla Black did. The most memorable catchphrase from the show was after the summary of each contestant by Graham or Tommy, which always concluded with, 'The choice is yours …'

Once the blind date choice had been made, the screen went back and the pair met for the very first time. The couple then picked an envelope that revealed where they would be jetting off to on their first date.

Each episode would then include a video diary of the couples who had been on their dates from the previous week's show. The couple would then join Cilla on the sofa for a chat about it all and to find out what they really thought about

each other. This really did add a good deal of reality comedy to the show. Very often one of the couple would be acting as if they were enjoying themselves but when facing the camera would come out with how they really felt about their blind date!

Long before internet dating and despite its longevity and theme of couples falling in love, there were in fact only three weddings as a result of the game show. Black was a guest at each of them and one of Black's memorable themes when a couple showed promise was about getting her hat out!

Blind Date was extremely popular with British audiences and during the 1980s it had some eighteen million viewers tuning in on a Saturday night.

Blockbusters

British game show Blockbusters was created by Steve Ryan and Mark Goodson and was first broadcast on ITV in 1983. It ran for a total of ten series and one thousand two hundred and four episodes on ITV until its final in 1993. Other television channels also broadcast the game show and in fact the last was broadcast by Thames Television Productions in 2012.

Presented by Bob Holness from 1983 the contestants had to answer trivia question to complete a joined up path across or down a game board of twenty interlocking hexagons arranged in five columns of four. Each hexagon contained a letter of the alphabet (apart from X and Z). One contestant competed against two others in a bid to prove whether the old adage of two heads are better than one was true.

Each contestant would pick a letter strategically and a question would be asked where the answer to it would begin with the corresponding letter chosen. Give me a 'P' please Bob became a ridiculous school playground catchphrase and pun.

The solo player had to connect four white hexagons vertically and the two-player team had to connect five blue hexagons horizontally. The board was designed in such a way that there had to be a winner, there could not be a tie. For every correct answer five pounds was awarded. If the team or player got a question right then they continued to have control of the board. If the answer was incorrect then the opposing team got a chance to answer the question. If both sides got it wrong then Bob would ask another question based on the same letter of the alphabet. The first

side to make the complete link of hexagons won the game. The first side to win two games won the match.

Everyone won a 'Blockbusters' Concise Oxford Dictionary and a sweatshirt in the original series.

The winner of the match went on to do the 'Gold Run'. If the two-player team had won, only one of them could play this. Similar to the hexagon pattern of the main game board, the player had to get answers correct to horizontally connect and they had sixty seconds to do it. If, however, they got an answer wrong that hexagon turned black not gold and would block their intended path. The

hexagons for the Gold Run also had two to four letters on instead of one. For example, if EE was shown the question might be, what chocolate gift is given at the end of Lent in the Christian calendar; answer Easter Egg.

The game show actually originated from the American game show of the same name, although it was much more popular in the United Kingdom. The format for the game show was so very popular that it was also replicated in Australia, Germany, France, Indonesia, Israel, Italy, the Netherlands, Paraguay, Sweden, Switzerland, Turkey and the United Arab Emirates.

Bob's Full House

Presented by Bob Monkhouse, Bob's Full House was a very popular quiz programme on BBC One and it ran for six series and one hundred and ten episodes from 1984 to 1990. Where else could you win some fabulous prizes!

The game show was based on the game of bingo and four contestants competed with each other to try and fill out their bingo-like card. This, however, was numbered from one to sixty and not one to ninety like a normal bingo house card. Before the game could commence, however, the game show always began with Bob Monkhouse giving a fairly lengthy stand-up comedy routine.

Once the game show was at last underway the four contestants had to answer questions correctly in order to try and get a full house ... or 'Bob's Full House'! If they got a question wrong,

however, they were 'wallied' and were therefore not allowed to even attempt answering the following question.

The first round was pretty basic and required a person to get four questions right in order for them to win the round and, yes, win a choice of prizes. Round two was the Monkhouse Mastercard where the players would try and light up the middle row. Contestants would be asked questions unopposed by the others, but if they got it wrong the other players were allowed to buzz in and answer. If the buzzer got it wrong then they would be 'wallied'.

The third and final round was very similar to the first, apart from the fact that the objective was to complete the remainder of the bingo card. The first person to achieve this won the game and had the chance to win a holiday in the following round, the

Gold Card bonus round.

The winning player had to face a board of eighteen squares with numbers from one to sixty on and stars on others. They had sixty seconds to answer a series of maximum fifteen questions. For every correct answer a number on the board was chosen that revealed an amount of money in pounds. Some of the numbers had letters too and if the player could guess the holiday destination by revealing them before the time ran out then they won that holiday. Nobody went home empty handed though, and despite Bob Monkhouse's famous efforts to help anyone win the holiday, when it didn't happen they went home with a hamper as a consolation prize.

Bullseye

Super, smashing, great! Created by Andrew Wood and Norman Vaughan, British game show Bullseye was originally broadcast on ITV from 1982 until 1995 and totalled sixteen series. It was presented by Jim Bowen and also starred the referee Tony Green. Many will remember those cold winter Sunday evenings when Bullseye became more than a game show, it was more like a British institution before the Monday morning work routine hit again.

Based on darts, three pairs of contestants, one of which was an amateur player and the other a complete novice player, would compete in three different rounds. The first round saw the darts player throw. The board was segmented into categories such as Pot Luck, Sport, History Showbiz etc. Different amounts of prize money was available for different parts of the board,

the easiest segments earning thirty pounds, right up to the bullseye that was worth two hundred pounds. The non-dart player would pick a segment and ideally the dart player would hit it to win the money. If a category not chosen was hit then they could answer the question but wouldn't get the cash for the throw, only for the question if answered correctly. For most of the series the lowest scoring couple would be eliminated from the show after this round.

Round two was Pounds for Points. The contestants threw three darts at a time at a traditional dart board and the points scored were converted to pounds if a general knowledge question was answered correctly. After three rounds of this the highest scoring pair went through to the next round. The losing players were given a set of darts, a tankard, a bendy Bully and the money that they had just won from the first two rounds. This always ended just before the ad break which would begin just as Jim began counting their money. He would say, 'take me two minutes … see you in a couple of throws!'

Straight after the adverts a professional darts player would then throw for a charity of the remaining contestants choice. If over 301 points were scored with nine darts, this was doubled. The final two rounds consisted of Bully's Prize Board, where the black and red segments meant winning prizes for hitting the smaller red segments. If hit twice though the prize was then lost. Hitting the bullseye meant winning 'Bully's Special Prize'. The Bully's Star Prize gamble finished the show and the pair had to decide whether to gamble their winnings for the mystery star prize hidden behind a screen. To win, the pair, with only six darts to throw, had to score 101 or more. When they failed they were shown the prize anyway with Jim saying 'come and have a look at what you could have won'!

The game show had many catchphrases that were well known amongst adults and children alike. 'Keep out of the black and in the red, nothing in this game for two

in a bed'; 'You win nothing but your BFH … bus fare home'; 'You've got the time it takes for the board to revolve …'; 'You can't beat a bit of Bully'; 'And Bully's Special prize …' Bring back a bit of nostalgia from those good old family Sunday evenings?!

Call My Bluff

Long-running British game show Call My Bluff was first broadcast on BBC Two from 1965 to 1994. It then returned on BBC One in 1996 and continued until 2005. It was the second British game show to be broadcast in colour.

The game show contestants consisted of two teams of three celebrities. Each team took it in turn to give three definitions of an obscure word, obviously only one of which was actually correct. Guess what, two were bluffs and one wasn't and it was the opposing team's job to guess which one was correct.

The two teams always had a captain and over the years they have included Frank Muir, Robert Morley, Alan Melville, Michael Flanders, Drusilla Beyfus, Kenneth Horne, Patrick Campbell, Arthur Marshall, Joanna Lumley, Alan Coren, Sandi Toksvig and Rod Liddle. One of the show's famous catchphrases was 'So now, let's meet our first captain – the man with the revolving bow tie – Frank Muir' and also, 'Now, we'll see if this bell still works (ding) – yes, it does, and it brings up our first word, which is …'

There were many different combinations of teams over the years that Call My Bluff was broadcast, but the best combination was arguably that in the era of Holness, Coren and Toksvig. This was because the two captains had a brilliant rapport with each other, making the show much more alive and entertaining. During this era some great guests also appeared (and on more than one occasion due to their popularity on the show). These included John Sergeant, Bill Paterson, Barry Cryer and Bernard Cribbins.

Toksvig was undoubtedly a larger than life character on the game show and she was often keen to use props and different styles of wordplay to define her words. She used puppets, mini-plays, in which she'd get Bob Holness to partake as the male part, not to mention getting Bob to get his old Blockbuster companion out on occasion – Harold the Hedgehog!

Over the years there were many presenters, some of whom are still very well known today. Originally, but only for the first year Call My Bluff was presented by Robin Ray. Joe Melia replaced him from 1966 for another year, when Peter Wheeler was hired for one more. It was Robert Robertson who became part of the furniture and he presented the game show from 1969 until 1988. Bob Holness was in charge from 1996 until 2003, Fiona Bruce took the helm for the final two years of the original second run and Angus Deayton presented a special episode in 2011.

Catchphrase

Created by Stephen Radosh the British ITV game show Catchphrase was first broadcast in 1986 and after nineteen series and three hundred and sixty-eight episodes, finally came to an end in 2002. In 2012 it was announced that a revived version of the show would be broadcast, which happened in April 2013. Catchphrase has now been commissioned for a second series in this revived format and it was first broadcast in March 2014.

The original series was presented by Roy Walker from 1986 to 1999, followed by Nick Weir from 2000 to 2002. Two contestants played (one male and one female) and the point was to win money by identifying a well-known and familiar phrase that was represented by an animation clip accompanied by background music. The show had a

mascot called Mr Chips who was a golden robot and he frequently starred in the animation clips of the catchphrases. Before each round of this, however, one player had to stop a flashing light. This would determine how much money each correct answer in that particular round was worth. Then the animated puzzle appeared in front of them and, once the bell had sounded and not before without penalty, it was first on the buzzers. If correct, the player won the money, which was accrued on the front of their red and blue playing stations.

After each animated puzzle, the player who answered correctly got to try answering the Bonus Catchphrase. This consisted of nine squares, one of which was picked and removed. If the contestant could guess the catchphrase from the bit of picture revealed then they would win whatever was in the Bonus Bank at the time. If they couldn't, the other player would then choose a square and try, but each time another square was removed the amount of money in the Bonus Bank reduced.

The fast moving Ready Money Round always came after the adverts and in this round there was no bell. The player who had accrued the most money by the end of the rounds went through to the final Super Catchphrase round. This consisted of a grid of twenty-five squares with letters that flashed up. Behind each was a Catchphrase. If they answered five correctly they won extra money. To win a holiday and spending money the player had to crack the 'M' square, which was supposed to be the difficult one.

Notably Catchphrase was one of the very first British game shows to make use of new technology of computer animations and it was seen as pretty cutting edge for mass market television at the time.

On Mother's Day in 2014 a celebrity special episode was broadcast and with their respective mothers it starred David Walliams, Emma Willis and Kimberley Walsh.

TELLY ADDICT : **GAME SHOWS**

Countdown

Created by French television producer Armand Jammot, British game show Countdown was actually the first programme to be broadcast on Channel 4 in 1982. Since then over five thousand episodes have been aired making it one of the longest-running game shows in the world. Based around word and number puzzles, Countdown became very popular very quickly with British television audiences and it has established a cult status in the country.

The game show first began with the words, 'As the countdown to a brand new channel ends, a brand new Countdown begins'. These were spoken by the original presenter Richard Whiteley, who presented the programme until his untimely death in 2005. Since then the presenters have been Des Lynam (2005 to 2006), Des O'Connor (2007 to 2008), Jeff Stelling (2009 to 2011) and the current presenter Nick Hewer.

Countdown's co-host for twenty-six years was British media personality Carol Jean Vorderman MBE. In fact it was because of her role on Countdown that she made such a name for herself. Television presenter Rachel Riley took over the role in 2009. The Countdown team is also enhanced by lexicographer and adjudicator Susie Dent who has been on the game show since 1992.

There are two contestants for each show, as well as a celebrity guest who features between the advert breaks. There are three different rounds that the contestants play: the ten letters round, the four numbers round, and the conundrum round. The winner of each show returns the next day and continues to do so until either beaten or eight wins are accrued.

The most successful contestants are then asked back to compete in the Countdown finals.

The letters round consists of two piles of letters; one with the consonants and one with the vowels. The contestant picks a total of nine letters, which must contain at least three vowels and four consonants. Both contestants then have thirty seconds to come up with the longest word possible using the letters displayed. One point is awarded per letter for the longest word, unless the contestant has used all nine letters and then the score is doubled.

The numbers round requires a contestant to pick six out of twenty-four shuffled number tiles that are set into two groups: four large numbers and two of each from one to ten. A random three-digit target is then computer generated and the contestants have thirty seconds to try and work out how to use the numbers picked to get to the target figure using addition, subtraction, multiplication and division.

The final round is the 'Countdown Conundrum'. A nine-letter anagram is revealed on the board and the contestants have thirty seconds to work out the nine-letter word. Quite often the letters are shown in the form of two condensed words just to make it a little bit more difficult.

In addition to the regular everyday Countdown programmes, there have been numerous special episodes and series. These include anniversary and birthday shows as well as a Master series, Celebrity series, Ladies' Championship, Junior Championship and Champion of Champions tournaments.

Crackerjack

British children's game show Crackerjack was created by John Downes and was first broadcast in 1955. It ran for twenty-nine series totalling four hundred and fifty-one episodes and only came to an end in December 1984.

'It's Friday, it's five to five … It's Crackerjack!' How many of us don't remember that?! Well, ok if you were born after 1980 you may not, but Crackerjack was an absolute firm favourite with generations of children and is one of those programmes that remains firmly etched in the nostalgic memory banks of childhood. It was originally broadcast on a Thursday, but moved to Friday allowing Blue Peter to have two weekday slots on Monday and Thursday.

The show was filmed at the BBC Television Theatre, which is now the Shepherds Bush Empire to an audience largely made up of children. Each forty-minute show comprised of a variety of fun and games. There were competitive games for children in teams, a music spot, some comedy acts and the finale, in which the cast performed a funny short play that incorporated popular songs of the day. Perhaps one of the most memorable games on the show was the quiz called 'Double or Drop'. Every time a contestant answered a question correctly they were given a prize to hold. If, however, they got the question wrong, they were given a cabbage to hold as well. They would be eliminated from the game if they dropped anything they were holding, or ended up with three cabbages. It seems a little mad now, but this part of Crackerjack enraptured generations of children for years!

Around 1977 a talent contest element was added to the show called 'Crackerjack

Young Entertainer of the Year'. Towards the end of the show's life, and in an attempt to boost waning viewing figures, a new game called 'Take a Chance' was introduced in 1982 and this involved gunge. Celebrity guests would team up with the children's teams and would be able to score points for them. The gunge would fall on them and/or Stu Francis (presenter at the time) if a question was answered incorrectly.

There were many presenters of Crackerjack over the years, many of whom are still household names: Eamonn Andrews from 1955 to 1964, Leslie Crowther from 1964 to 1968, Michael Aspel from 1968 to 1974, Ed Stewart from 1975 to 1979 and Stu Francis from 1980 to 1984.

The programme also had regular personalities for certain sections of the show as well as celebrity guest appearances. Peter Glaze and Don Maclean provided early comedy sketches, as did Ronnie Corbett, Leslie Crowther, Bernie Clifton, Little and Large and The Krankies. Later series featured Basil Brush, and magic was performed by 'The Great Soprendo' (Geoffrey Durham). Singers and dancers also helped to host the games and the likes of Petula Clark and Julie Borne-Brown were amongst them.

Unfortunately, only one hundred and forty-eight out of four hundred and fifty-one episodes of Crackerjack have survived in the BBC archives.

Deal or No Deal

Created by Dick de Rijk, game show Deal or No Deal originated in the Netherlands, was called Miljoenenjacht or Hunt for Millions and was produced by Dutch producer Endemol in 2000. It is broadcast all over the world today. In the United Kingdom Deal or No Deal is presented by Noel Edmonds and has been broadcast for nine series since 2005.

Featuring a single contestant who has to try and beat The Banker, the game is a simple one of chance and nerve. There are now twenty-three (used to be twenty-two) identical sealed red boxes each containing randomly chosen sums of money ranging from one pence to two hundred and fifty thousand pounds, and now even a possible half a million pounds thanks to very recent changes. Twenty-three contestants are present

at the start, each stand behind one of the red boxes and only the adjudicator knows what value of money is in what box. At the start of each game only one of the contestants are chosen to play.

With Edmonds serving as the game co-ordinator and the middleman with the unseen Banker who he speaks to on the telephone, the contestant moves with their box to the 'pound table' in the centre of the set.

Different boxes are opened over several rounds and the objective of the game is for the contestant to try and win the highest amount of money possible, but The Banker is offering them deals and wants to pay out as little as possible at the end of the day. Of course it is better if the contestant selects boxes with smaller amounts of money, so that these can be eliminated from the game, leaving the possibility of higher amounts in the remaining boxes. Once the required numbers of boxes have been opened in a round, The Banker offers to buy the contestant's original box (that hasn't been opened). The contestant has to consider the offer and decide what to do, answering with either 'deal' or 'no deal'.

If 'no deal' is given, then play continues until only two boxes remain. If the final offers from The Banker are still rejected then the contestant goes home with the amount in their original box. If 'deal' is chosen then the contestant agrees to take the offer from The Banker and gives up the right to the money in their original box. When this happens a hypothetical outcome is played out to reveal what would have happened if the contestant had said 'no deal'.

Deal or No Deal has been syndicated all over the world and is broadcast in over seventy countries from Afghanistan to Vietnam. Each country has it's own version of the game and also own top prize value. Only a handful of contestants have ever won the top prize on any version of the game show. For this to happen, the contestant would first have to choose the case containing the top prize (a four to five per cent chance

depending on the number of amounts in the game), and then would have to reject every single offer that the banker proposes during the game.

Double Your Money

Double Your Money was a British quiz show that was first broadcast on Radio Luxembourg. It then moved to being aired on ITV in 1955, a few days after the television channel started broadcasting. Hosted by presenter Hughie Green, the quiz show ran for two hundred and sixty thirty-minute episodes until 1968.

The Monday night quiz involved a contestant choosing a subject category and then answering questions on that subject. One pound was won for the first correct answer and then for every correct answer after that the money was doubled up to a maximum of thirty-two pounds. If the contestant answered a question incorrectly they would lose everything they had accrued to that point. The most successful players went on to play for the Treasure Trail and could win up to one thousand pounds.

The choice of subject categories were the same for each series, but did evolve and change over time and included subjects like Astronomy, Chemistry, Cricket, Cooking, English History, Films, Football, General Knowledge, Good Housekeeping, Law (Criminal), Literature, Music, Music Hall, Painting, Theatre and Zoology, to name a few.

The first contestant to enter the Treasure Trail was a Mr Plantagenet Somerset Fry and he became a celebrity overnight. Former Oxford University post-graduate, he ended up with five hundred and twelve pounds, deciding not to risk it all for the one thousand pound jackpot. The first winner of the jackpot was a young female student called Robin Burke and won by answering questions on Chaucer's Canterbury Tales.

In the early days, Hughie Green would be introduced by the hostess thus, 'We'd like you to meet the man with the biggest head in television, the man with the greenest hue … Hughie Green!' One of the hostesses was the future Dame Maggie Smith who was only twenty years old at the time. She didn't stay on the show for long, however, as her acting career was just beginning to take off and she landed a role on Broadway only a few months into the programme's run. Other former hostesses included Valerie Drew, an elderly cleaner and former contestant Alice Earrey, Nancy Roberts, Julie de Marco, and Monica Rose, who had also appeared on the show as a fifteen-year-old accounts clerk. Hughie Green took so much of a shine to Monica that not only did she become a host on Double Your Money, but also for Green's sequel show The Sky's the Limit.

Eggheads

BBC quiz show Eggheads was first broadcast in 2003 and is still a very popular British programme. It has so far reached fourteen series and one thousand two hundred and ninety episodes at the time of writing.

The aim of the game is for a team of five amateur quizzers (usually with an obscure team name) to take on the five quiz professionals (the Eggheads) to win as much prize money as possible. In the first four rounds the challengers are given a category and must decide which one of them will take it and which of the Eggheads they want to take on for the challenge. If the challengers have done their homework diligently, they will already know what the weaknesses are of each particular Egghead, so this can be played to their advantage if they are smart. No conferring with the team is allowed, so the selected players are moved to a 'question room' and shown on a large screen. Each player (the challenger and the Egghead) is given three multiple-choice questions and whoever gets the most correct wins the duel. Any ties are dealt with by sudden death questions. Losing the duel also has the consequence of that player being eliminated from the all-important final round.

The remainder of the team who have not lost a duel then face the Eggheads in the final round. It is in the same three multiple-choice question format as the previous rounds, but this time the teams are allowed to confer on the answers. Again, any ties are broken by sudden death questions. If the challengers win then they get the jackpot money.

The nine possible subjects in the head-to-head rounds are: Arts and Books,

Film and Television, Food and Drink, Geography, History, Music, Politics, Science and Sport. Prior to 2008 Music and Film and Television were under a single category of Entertainment.

The team of Eggheads includes or has included Kevin Ashman, Daphne Fowler, Chris Hughes, Judith Keppel, Barry Simmons, Pat Gibson, Dave Rainford and CJ de Mooi. All of the Eggheads are quiz champions in their own right and are winners of shows such as Fifteen to One, Mastermind, Who Wants to Be a Millionaire, World Quizzing Championships etc. The Eggheads team rotates in each episode so that only five are playing at any one time.

Every day that the Eggheads are not beaten in the final round by the challenging team, the prize money goes up by one thousand pounds. Since the quiz show began, and at the time of writing, one hundred and five teams have managed to beat the Eggheads and the amount of prize money the BBC has paid out now exceeds one million pounds. The record win stands with a team of students from Oxford Brookes University called 'Beer Today, Gone Tomorrow' and they won seventy-five thousand pounds.

Every Second Counts

Hosted by Paul Daniels, Every Second Counts was a game show that was broadcast on BBC One between 1986 and 1993. In total nine series culminating in one hundred and forty-one episodes were aired. It was produced in association with Talbot Television and Group W Productions and the concept for the show originated from a United States version of the same name.

The name of the game was to win seconds of time (as opposed to points or monetary amounts). Each week three married couples would compete against each other. The games were split so that for each round only one half of the couple were allowed to answer the question and were 'in the driving seat'. The questions were all statements and each had two possible answers. For every correct answer given, the couple would earn more seconds. If an answer was incorrect then that player was eliminated from the round. There was a choice of two categories of questions for each round and the first round of questions earned two seconds per correct answer, this was doubled in the second half of the game show to four seconds. Perhaps most hilarious during this part of the game show was actually the facial expressions of the silent partner in a couple, when obviously not allowed to speak, their other half was struggling to choose the correct answer!

Both halves of the game also gave the contestants the opportunity to increase their time accrued by up to ten seconds in the bonus round. Each couple, starting with the couple sitting in last place, would be asked to choose a category and then a question was asked. They could give as many answers as they liked in the ten seconds allowed until they got the answer correct. The remaining (if any) time would then be added to their score. At the end of the first two rounds, the couple with the most seconds went through to the final round and the other two couples went home with a pair of Every Second Counts watches and an Every Second Counts clock.

The final round was so that the winning couple to try and win prizes by using the time they had won during the show. Having chosen one category out of two, they would have to complete a statement. Each correct answer given would extinguish a light. The first four lights meant first prize, then five lights gave them second prize and six for third prize. A holiday could be won if seven lights were extinguished. Only two prizes could be won, however. This caused some confusion; the first prize was kept automatically, but for five, six or seven lights, the prize just increased in value, they weren't all up for grabs.

The two announcers for the show were Phillip Talbot and later Jonathan Booth and the beginning of the show would begin with the announcement,

'And here's your host for Every ... Second ... Counts, Pauuuul Daniels!'. Other famous catchphrases from the game show included 'Are you all ready to play? Say yes Paul!' and 'No help from the back, please!'

Family Fortunes

Based on the American game show Family Feud, Family Fortunes was the British version and it originally ran from 1980 until 2002 culminating in twenty-two series and five hundred and twenty-four episodes. Apart from being one of the longest-running game shows in the country, during its peak years, Family Fortunes was also one of television's highest rated game shows and it was adored by millions of families every week throughout the country.

The presenters of Family Fortunes included comedian Bob Monkhouse from 1980 to 1980, singer and entertainer Max Bygraves from 1983 to 1985, comedian and actor Les Dennis from 1987 to 2002, and Andy Collins for the remainder of the programme in 2002 when it was moved to a daytime slot. It only had a short run as such before the format was axed altogether. Revived episodes are also currently being shown on ITV under the title All Star Family Fortunes; this is and has been presented by Vernon Kay since 2006 and consists of four family members plus one celebrity on each side.

The original game show revolved around two family teams of five members competing against each other. They were lined up either side of their host and faced the large computer screen on which the answers and results were revealed, along with some now iconic noises, such as the computerised 'Eh-uh' sound that was used when an answer was wrong.

The questions asked were all based on the results of surveys and the famous catchphrase was, 'we asked one hundred people to …' One nominated person from each family would then hit the buzzer at the podium to guess, ideally, what the top answer was first time. If not the top answer then the opposing family were allowed to guess. Whichever family won then got to play or pass the round. Mostly they played and then the rest of the family took it in turns to guess the other answers. With three incorrect answers and the famous cross and 'Eh-uh', the round passed over to the opposing family. They only had to guess one more to win all the money accrued to that point. This was then followed after the adverts by exactly the same, but this time they could double their money.

Whichever family reached three hundred pounds first went through to the final Big Money round where the tension and excitement really climaxed! Two members were then selected to play the fast money game against the clock. The first player had to answer five questions within fifteen seconds, then the second player (who was put in a booth with headphones) had twenty seconds to complete the missing answers. If they got to two hundred points or more from the ten possible answers they won the top cash prize.

The large computer screen was affectionately named Mr Babbage by Bob Monkhouse and was done so in

recognition of Charles Babbage, the English mathematician, philosopher, inventor and mechanical engineer who came up with the concept of a programmable computer.

Fifteen to One

Created by John M. Lewis and first broadcast on Channel 4 in 1988, Fifteen to One was a very popular quiz game show that originally ran until 2003. It has since been revived as a daytime programme and in total has been broadcast for thirty-seven series, totalling two thousand three hundred and fifty episodes at the time of writing.

Presented by William G. Stewart for its entire original run, the quiz show was based on fifteen contestants standing in a semi-circle facing Stewart. Each contestant started the show with three lives and the idea was not to lose any lives by getting any questions wrong.

The first round consisted of each contestant in turn being asked a general knowledge question in two rounds. If they got one wrong they lost a life, but if they got both wrong they were eliminated from the game immediately.

The second round was slightly different and at this point each contestant would have had two or three lives remaining. As in the first round the contestants were asked questions in turn and again, one life would be lost for an incorrect answer. As soon as a player answered correctly, however, they could then nominate who the following question would be directed at. If they got this wrong, they would lose a life and the player who had chosen them would then choose another player. Whoever then answered correctly won the opportunity to do the nominating. This continued until only three contestants were left standing.

Round three and the final was played for points. Each player was restored to full life with three reinstated and after the first few series, if a player had finished

the second round with one, two or three lives in tact, this would be rewarded in corresponding bonus points going into the next round, therefore giving the person who was doing the best to have a slight advantage going into the final.

After a player introduction, the final began and up to forty questions were asked. Wrong answers cost lives and again, three lives lost meant instant elimination, regardless of points scored. The first question was on the buzzer and again, once a correct answer had been given the play reverted to the nominate a player format. The winner would be either the last person standing, or in the event of all forty questions being answered and more than one player standing, the player with

the most points won. For every life left at this point ten points were added to the final score. Every season also had a Grand Final but the final round of this was all done on the buzzer.

At the beginning of the thirty-fifth and final original series, William G. Stewart read out the statistics that the programme had clocked up, which included nearly three hundred and fifty thousand questions being asked to thirty-three thousand nine hundred and seventy-five contestants. It is also worthy of note that William G. Stewart (full name William Gladstone Stewart as he was occasionally introduced as) also produced the quiz show and helped write some of the questions, particularly the historical ones.

Give Us a Clue

Running for nearly twenty years, Give Us a Clue was a hugely popular British game show that was based on the game of charades. It was broadcast on ITV from 1979 to 1992.

The two teams had captains of which actor and television presenter Lionel Blair was one and actor and former dancer Una Stubbs was the other. Stubbs was replaced by actress Liz Goddard as captain of the women's team in later episodes of the game show. The presenters were famously Michael Aspel from 1979 to 1984 and Michael Parkinson from 1984 to 1992.

Give Us a Clue was basically a televised game of charades (a word guessing game) in which different well-known personalities from television, sport etc. joined the team captains to try and out charade each other. For those who haven't ever had the pleasure in playing it, charades is a party game that requires one person to mime and not utter a word, a name, phrase, book, play film or television programme. Charades requires a combination of ingenuity, personal flamboyance and acting skills, as well as using specific and particular sign language to mean definite things, an aspect of the game that has evolved over the years such as touching ones ear to represent 'sounds like' or making a box shape with ones fingers to represent a television programme.

In Give Us a Clue, each player was given the subject or name of their charade by the presenter and then they had approximately two minutes to act out their given subject in front of their team. If they guessed in the first minute they got three points and two points if guessed correctly in the second minute. If they didn't guess the charade correctly in the allotted time it was then offered over to the opposing team, which gave them a bonus point.

There were certainly some hilarious moments when on occasion the charade given would be either totally absurd or ridiculously long and obscure such as a twenty-four word long song title or as one of Michael Parkinson's cards read, the 'A-Z of horse diseases and health problems, signs, diagnoses, causes, treatment' – Lionel Blair was on the receiving end of that little Parky gem!

In the early days of the game show it was popular enough to command a weekday early evening slot, but by 1987 it was moved to an early morning slot, which was probably the start of its demise.

There was an attempt to revive the show in 1997 when Tim Clark presented it alongside team captains, actor and screenwriter Christopher Blake and actress Julie Peasgood, but it only ran for thirty episodes. In 2011 Give Us a Clue did return for a Comic Relief special episode and it included Sara Cox, Christopher Biggins, Lionel Blair, Una Stubbs, Holly Walsh, Jenni Falconer and David Walliams.

Going for Gold

British television game show Going for Gold was first broadcast on BBC One between 1987 and 1996 totalling seven hundred and three episodes over ten series. It was presented for the entire original run by Irish broadcaster Henry Kelly and was always aired straight after the lunchtime broadcast of the Australian soap opera Neighbours. The game show was then revived in 2008 on Channel 5 and was hosted by newsreader John Suchet. This version of Going for Gold was broadcast live, but it only lasted for one season, just over a hundred episodes and came to an end in 2009.

Going for Gold consisted of four rounds daily and then the winner of the final round was put through to the end of week finals. The winner of this every week was then put through to later stages of the series. So, every day one contestant out of seven went through to the final day and the remaining contestants returned each subsequent day. Therefore, by the Thursday show only four contestants would be left.

The opening round started with some short general knowledge questions being fired at all the contestants. From here, only four out of the seven would go through to the next 'first proper round' and it was the first four who answered four questions correctly. The format of these questions was usually something like 'Who am I?', followed by a short description by Kelly and the contestants had to guess.

Round two was the beat the buzzer round, again general knowledge questions were asked, which were worth one, two or three points. When a contestant got a question right, after being told the subject of the next, they would assign one, two or three points to it. The first three players to reach six points went through to round three.

Out of a choice of four categories, the remaining three players had to pick a category. The first player to get through got first pick of the categories. Each then had forty seconds to answer questions on their chosen subject. Points accrued based on how quickly they answered (between one and four points). If, however, they got the question wrong their score went back to zero. The final score for each was based on the highest point that they reached during the forty seconds. The highest two players went through to the final round.

Again, questions were worth one to four points in the final round depending on how quickly they were answered correctly. The format of questions was the same as the first round 'Who am I?' or 'What am I?' etc. One contestant played at a time in time segments but if they gave an incorrect answer, their remaining time and question would be passed to the other player. The winner

of the day was the first to score nine points and went through to Friday's final.

It's a Knockout

It's a Knockout was a British game show that originated from the French game show Intervilles that was created by French game show host and producer Maurice Guy, better known as Guy Lux. The British version of It's a Knockout was first broadcast on BBC One in 1966. It originally ran on BBC One weekly until 1982, thereafter only special episodes were broadcast until 1988. The game show then returned on Channel 5 this time and ran from 1999 to 2001. There was also a Welsh version called Gemau Heb Ffiniau or Games Without Frontiers and this was broadcast between 1991 and 1994.

The format of It's a Knockout was basically outside antics where teams were made up of a group of people from a particular town or city competing against another. More often than not the game show was played outside at a town's park for example where the local population would turn up whatever the weather to support their side. Bearing in mind our wonderful British weather, it was not uncommon for the grassy space chosen to quickly turn into a mud bath, making the games even more difficult for the contestants, but obviously pretty hilarious for the on-looking soggy audience all huddled under umbrellas or wearing pack a macs!

The actual games played in It's a Knockout, looking back now, were totally absurd in fact. Described as school sports day for adults, most of them required the adult team members to compete wearing enormous large foam rubber costumes. Points were won depending on which team won a particular challenge and a team could double their points in any one

round by playing their 'joker'. Arthur Ellis, an international football referee, refereed all the games.

Most of the games incorporated something wet and slippery, whether that was water, custard pies, greasy poles, rolling wet logs or simply a big blow-up swimming pool. The teams would be told what their task was, climbing a greasy pole or picking up eggs with an industrial excavator for example, and all attempted in the ridiculous (usually grotesque looking) enormous foam costumes.

The game show was not complicated; basically the team that won the most points went through to the next stage. The winning team won an It's a Knockout trophy and were given the chance to represent the United Kingdom in the European finals of the European-wide television game show, Jeux Sans Frontières (Games Without Frontiers).

Several presenters hosted It's a Knockout over the years. For the first year McDonald Hobley was in charge, then from 1967 to 1971 David Vine took over, followed by Stuart Hall from 1972 to 1988. The Channel 5 version was presented by Keith Chegwin and Lucy Alexander between 1999 and 2001.

In addition to the European-wide game of Jeux Sans Frontières, the format of the game show was also popular in Australia and New Zealand, also as It's a Knockout, plus the United States as Almost Anything Goes.

Mastermind

British quiz show Mastermind is a very long-running show for which it is renowned for its high level of intensity, challenging, difficult questions and intimidating setting. Created by producer Bill Wright, Mastermind first entered British television audience lives in 1972. The inspiration for the show and the famous black leather chair in which the contestants sit under a spotlight came from Wright's experiences during World War II when he was interrogated by the Gestapo. Since its inception, the basic format of Mastermind has never changed.

Mastermind has run for twenty-five series on BBC One, most famously presented by Magnus Magnusson; it ran until 1997 on BBC One. The original black chair was presented to Magnus Magnusson as a retirement present. Peter Snow presented the show on BBC Radio 4 that ran from 1998 to 2000. Clive Anderson took the reigns for a series of Mastermind broadcast between 2001 and 2002 on the Discovery Channel. Since 2003, returning to the BBC but this time on BBC Two, John Humphrys has presented the show that is still broadcast and has so far reached ten series.

Although now there is a little more interaction and information given about each contestant compared with the original series', the basic format of the show remains the same. Four and later five contestants sit on a row of chairs. One by one they are invited up to sit in the famous black chair, the lights are dimmed and the spotlight is put on them. The first round is on the contestant's chosen specialised subject and they then have two minutes to answer as many questions as possible. Contestants can pass to move onto the next question more quickly. One point is scored for each correct answer given. Incorrect answers are corrected by the presenter at the time, whereas any passes are answered at the end of the two minutes. Each contestant has their two minutes in the chair one after the other.

Each contestant can choose any specialised subject, such as 'The life and works of Shakespeare', 'The Moomin saga by Tove Jansson' and 'The history of Lancashire County Cricket Club'.

At the end of the first round the scores are announced in reverse order. For the second and final round the contestants are invited up to the chair in reverse order, so the lowest scoring contestant sits in the chair first. This is a general knowledge round and (if they are good at it) is an opportunity to make up some points and places. The winner is quite simply the person who has the most points.

The total number of passes for each contestant is also taken into consideration in the event of a tie. The contestant with the least number of passes in this situation beats the other. The winner goes through to the next round until the finals at the end of each series. A new specialised subject is required for every appearance on the show.

The highest ever score on Mastermind was achieved by English quiz player Kevin Ashman who has been an Egghead since 2003. Ashman scored forty-one points in 1995 with a specialised subject on 'The Life of Martin Luther King'. He went on to become the IQA champion (World Quizzing Championship) four times and also holds the highest ever score on Brain of Britain.

Other spin-off shows of Mastermind have also been broadcast over the years including Celebrity Mastermind, International Mastermind, Junior Mastermind and Sport Mastermind.

Name That Tune

Created by Harry Salter in 1976, Name That Tune was a British television game show during which two contestants competed against each other with regard to their knowledge of songs. The game show originally ran on ITV until 1988. It was then revived on Channel 5 from 1997 to 1998.

The British television version of Name That Tune originated from a radio show that was aired on NBC Radio in the United States in 1952. When the British version was first broadcast on television it was given a fifteen-minute slot on the popular entertainment series Wednesday At Eight. Due to its popularity with television audiences the producers, Thames Television, decided to turn Name That Tune into its own thirty-minute weekly series in 1983.

British actor and comedian Tom O'Connor hosted the show from 1976 to 1983. British actor, choreographer, tap dancer and television presenter Lionel Blair then took over and hosted the game show until the end of its original run in 1988. When the series was revived in 1997 on Channel 5, English pianist, bandleader, singer, composer and television presenter Jules Holland took the reigns for the two series that were broadcast.

The original game, from 1983 to 1988, saw two contestants compete in a variety of different games in order to win points and cash prizes. The first game was called 'Melody Roulette'. There was a wheel on stage with varying sums of money, ranging from twenty-five pounds to one hundred pounds, which determined the value of identifying a tune correctly. The outer section of the wheel had two spaces with 'Double' on it and

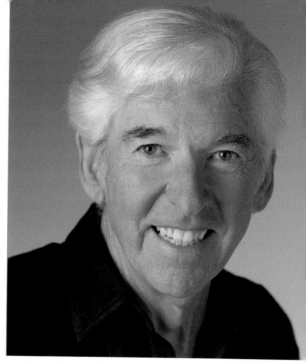

this was spun in the opposite direction. The first contestant to identify three tunes correctly out of five won the round.

Next was 'Sing a Note'. A tune was sung by the show's vocalist and the contestants had to write down the name of the tune. If any lyrics were a part of the song title, the singer would replace them with 'la-las'. Three tunes were sung in total for this round.

Only helped by a clue read out by the host, this round is famously remembered by the phrase 'I can name that tune in x notes'. This was the 'Bid a Note' round in which the contestants would outbid each other on how many notes they thought they could hear before guessing the name of the tune correctly. Obviously the fewer notes bid would win if answered correctly. The bidding ended and the round began when one contestant challenged the other to 'Name That Tune'. The first contestant to answer three correctly won the round.

The 'Golden Medley Showdown' was a buzzer round in which the contestants had to identify as many tunes as possible in thirty seconds. After all of these rounds the highest scoring contestant went on to the final, 'Prize Tune' round.

Put in an isolation booth where they could only hear the host and the piano, a golden envelope was opened to reveal the song as sheet music, which was handed to the pianist. The contestant only had one shot at getting this answer. They were given twenty seconds of piano playing and then had ten seconds to give the host the song's exact title. Once out of the booth, the host then revealed if it was correct or not. If it was, contestants usually won prizes such as a new car.

Opportunity Knocks

Originally a radio programme broadcast on the BBC Light Programme in 1949, later moving to Radio Luxembourg in the 1950s, Opportunity Knocks became a British television talent show that first ran on ITV for only a couple of months in 1956. ABC and then Thames broadcast the show between 1964 and 1978. The BBC then revived it in 1987 and that version of the show ran until 1990.

British television presenter Hughie Green hosted Opportunity Knocks from 1949 right through to 1978. English entertainer Bob Monkhouse then took the helm for the BBC from 1987 to 1989 and during this time the show was known as 'Bob Says Opportunity Knocks'. Comedian Les Dawson then took over for the final year of the show.

The format of the show was a very early version of what was to come in the twenty-first century with the likes of Britain's Got Talent. The most important factor about both of these shows is that the voting is done by the viewing public and not a panel of judges.

How archaic it now seems, but the early series' of Opportunity Knocks relied on the British television audiences sending in postal votes for their favourite contestant each week, the winner of each episode was then revealed the week later. When the BBC revived the show in 1987 with Bob Monkhouse as the presenter, it was the very first show that initiated audience telephone voting, something which is now very common place of course. Although it didn't count towards the final vote, both the early and BBC versions of Opportunity Knocks also used an audience clap o meter during the show.

Opportunity Knocks saw many different acts on its stage and often, because of relying on the public vote for the decision, the outcome was somewhat affected by the act, where because of something really silly or novel, the public would vote for it instead of voting for a contestant who really did show some natural talent. Perhaps the most famous example of this was when a young Su Pollard (British comedy actress famous for her roles in British sitcoms Hi-de-Hi! and You Rang, M'Lord), was beaten by a singing dog!

No different from some of the more modern stars who's careers are being launched by the talent shows that are now on television, Opportunity Knocks can also boast a now celebrated and famous alumni. To name a few, these include Freddie Star, Paul Daniels, Bonnie Langford, Les Dawson, Roy 'Chubby' Brown, Little and Large, Frank Carson. Perhaps one of the most famous personalities they got wrong and rejected at the first audition for the show was Lee Evans who tried to enter in 1986!

Play Your Cards Right

Based on the American game show known as Card Sharks, Play Your Cards Right was a British television game show that was created by the American producer Chester Feldman. Produced by London Weekend Television and first broadcast on ITV in 1980, Play Your Cards Right ran for sixteen series, totalling two hundred and forty-eight episodes until 2003, although there were years when the game show stopped. The first run was from 1980 to 1987; a more modern version was then broadcast from 1994 to 1999. Another and final revival was then produced in 2002.

Also known as 'Bruce Forsyth's Play Your Cards Right', guess what, the game show was presented by Sir Bruce Forsyth CBE during its entire run over the years. Forsyth became a British television household name due to hosting games shows such as this, and

for Play Your Cards Right he had particular catchphrases for which he became famous, such as 'It's nice to see you, to see you nice', with the audience always joining in for the final 'nice'. Also, 'You don't get anything for a pair, not in this game' and 'It's a Brucie bonus!'

The format of the show was based on big, oversized playing cards that were displayed on big boards. Couples alternated to answer questions (the answer of which was all based on surveys of a hundred people). The first couple would say how many out of a hundred gave a particular answer to a question and the opposing couple would decide whether to guess higher or lower. If the second couple were right they would get control of the cards, otherwise the first couple played.

With an ace being the highest and

two being the lowest, five cards were laid out. The basic principle of the game was to guess if the next card was higher or lower than the previous one. There were opportunities for the other couple to take over or a couple could 'freeze' their cards at certain points in a game. The winner was the couple who got to the end of the row of cards first. In the event of three questions being answered incorrectly on the last card, there was a sudden death to determine the outcome of the game.

The Brucie Bonus came in during the 1990s version of the show, which was awarded to the winner of each of the two games in the first half. The first couple to win two games became the overall winner. The winning couple then went on to play for cash prizes. Starting with two hundred points, they'd win an extra fifty for a correct question but lose fifty for an incorrect answer. The final game was played out the same as before, but there were two rows of three cards dealt out and one final card at the top. The maximum possible amount of money that could be won was over seventeen thousand pounds. The highest amount ever won in the show's history was nine and a half thousand pounds.

Ready Steady Cook

Daytime television cooking game show Ready Steady Cook was first broadcast on BBC One in 1994 and it originally ran until 2000. The show then moved to BBC Two for another ten years with a total of twenty-one series and a staggering one thousand seven hundred and thirty-five episodes over the first sixteen years. In addition to the everyday show, there have also been nine celebrity series of one hundred and two episodes and a further twenty-two special episodes.

For the first six years of Ready Steady Cook the game show was presented by Fern Britton and meeting celebrity chef Phil Vickery during the series, eventually married him in 2000. For the following ten years of the programme British celebrity chef and then television presenter Ainsley Harriott took the reigns.

Every day two different people joined two celebrity chefs in the studio kitchen. The contestants had five pounds with which to buy a bag of ingredients. Each team was designated a name, either 'red tomato' or 'green pepper'. Occasionally the budget for the bag was increased to seven pounds fifty, which was called the 'Bistro Bag', and when the budget was increased to ten pounds this was referred to as the 'Gourmet Bag'. A 'Lucky Dip' bag was also used sometimes. Containing ten food items, each team picked five out of the bag. The celebrity chefs were always chuffed to bits if they happened to be on for an increased budget bag as it often gave them much more luxurious ingredients to work with.

With the help of the contestants, some of whom were pretty useless in the kitchen, the chefs had twenty minutes

to prepare several dishes using only the ingredients in the bag, plus the larder that contained basic ingredients, herbs and spices. Once the twenty minutes was up each contestant tasted all of the dishes prepared and the chef usually gave the dishes a name (often a pun or comic name). Once all of the dishes on both sides had been tasted the vote went to the studio audience to decide which team had done the most inventive cooking with the ingredients they had to work with. The audience either held up a card with a red tomato or a green pepper to vote. These were then counted and the winning team announced. The winning contestant won a cash prize of one hundred pounds, which the celebrity chef donated to a charity of the contestant's choice. Originally the runner-up won a hamper, but as budget constraints set in over time, this became a Ready Steady Cook mug!

There were many celebrity chefs that participated in Ready Steady Cook over the years. Some of the most well known chefs included Ed Baines, James Martin, Nick Nairn, Paul Rankin, Tony Tobin, Brian Turner, Phil Vickery, Lesley Water, Kevin Woodford and Antony Worrall Thompson.

Red or Black?

British television game show Red or Black? was created by television personality Simon Cowell and it was first broadcast on ITV in 2011. Presented by the comedy duo from Newcastle upon Tyne, Ant and Dec (Anthony McPartlin and Declan Donnelly), Red or Black? Had a budget of fifteen million pounds and therefore became the most expensive game show in the history of television. The show ran for two series and fourteen episodes, coming to an end a year later.

Over one hundred thousand members of the public applied to be on the game show, out of which only eight contestants per live show were selected. Each episode consisted of ten rounds with those rounds being split up into three stages. The hopeful contestants started at Wembley Arena, the winners of this stage then moved to a particular location stage, and here the

numbers were reduced to the eight required for each episode of the game show. The show was then broadcast live from a live studio with the final eight contestants.

Rounds consisted of a wide variety of unusual activities such as the celebrity guests trying to hit a gong in the middle of a lake with a golf ball from a hundred yards away, and one of them being shot into the air on a reverse bungee.

The locations for the game show were varied and included Battersea Power Station, Thorpe Park, Alnwick Castle, the set for Coronation Street, and Eastnor Castle. Red or Black? also featured celebrity guests and the likes of David Hasselhoff, One Direction and Jedward (John and Edward Grimes), Rory McIlroy and Lee Westwood all appeared on the show to help contestants in the round where the contestants had

to choose red or black in order to get through to the following round.

The 'Duel' round, which was the penultimate, consisted of digitally displayed disc that had random sections of red and black, each colour having four sections, with the choice being hidden to the players. Randomly a player chose a colour leaving the other colour to the other player. Taking it in turns to then choose a number, the corresponding section of the disc was shown to the players and audience. The player to reach the final round was the first to reveal all four sections.

A giant roulette wheel split into thirty-six alternating red and black sections was used for the final round. If the player chose the correct colour Red or Black? they won a million pound prize. Four contestants became millionaires during the series, but the game show was not a critical success and did not become popular with British audiences, hence it only lasting for two series in total over only one year.

Robot Wars

Created by Tom Gutteridge and Steve Carsey, Robot Wars was a British game show that originated from the United States version of the game show with the same name. Broadcast on BBC Two between 1998 and 2003, the original series ran for seven series, totalling one hundred and twenty-one episodes. An Extreme two series was also broadcast totalling thirty episodes. The final series was broadcast on Channel 5.

The basic idea of the game show was for teams, made up of amateur and professional roboteers, to design and make a robot that would then fight against other teams' robots. In addition to fighting each other, the teams also had to avoid the 'House Robots'. These were not bound by the same weight or weapon limit restrictions as the team robots were.

Each episode of Robot Wars consisted of several rounds of challenges. In the first and second series this consisted of a group of six robots competing in six heats, the six heat champions then fought to determine the overall winner. The challenges consisted of the first 'The Gauntlet' challenge, which was a maze filled with obstacles and defended by house robots. The second challenge was called 'The Trial'. The games in this challenge varied from heat to heat but included trials such as 'British Bulldog', 'Labyrinth', 'Stock Car' and 'Football'. 'The Arena' was the third challenge in which four remaining robots were paired off. They then fought head-to-head to leave two winning robots to fight it out for the heat championship.

The Third Wars and Fourth Wars eliminated 'The Gauntlet' and 'The Trial' rounds from the main game

and instead focused on 'The Arena' format for competition. The result of which meant that the show became a knockout tournament. Several special shows were also shown during the third and fourth series including The First World Championship, The International League Championship, Celebrity Robot Wars and War of Independence. The last tournament saw the best of the British take on the best of the American roboteers.

The Fifth, Sixth and Seventh Wars followed a similar format to the former three series, but tweaks and changes were made over time. The Robot Wars Extreme series' featured various battles from competitions competed over the entire series. The first series focused on a headline battle at the end of each show, whereas the second series rather focused on single events.

The presenters of Robot Wars included British broadcaster and motoring journalist Jeremy Clarkson, television and radio presenter, producer and author Phillippa Forrester, Red Dwarf and Coronation Street actor Craig Charles and television presenters Julia Reed and Jayne Middlemiss. In addition to the presenters was the voice of British football commentator Jonathan Pearce.

Strike it Lucky

Presented by English comedian and television presenter Michael Barrymore, Strike it Lucky was a very popular British television game show that was broadcast between 1986 and 1999. The game show ran for fourteen series in total culminating in two hundred and five episodes. An updated version of the show was devised in its later stages and from 1996 Strike it Lucky changed its name to Strike it Rich.

The basic format of the show revolved around three teams of two contestants battling it out to win both cash and other prizes. With ten television monitors set in an arch shape across the stage, the idea was for each team to move across the television by answering questions. At the beginning of a contestant's go, they were given a subject category that had six possible corresponding answers. The

contestant decided how many answers to give (two, three of four) in order to move along the monitors corresponding to that number. If answered incorrectly the opposing team got the opportunity to answer correctly and take the moves.

As the players moved across the archway of television, the televisions revealed either a prize or a 'Hot Spot', all except for the last one that is. If a contestant landed on a monitor that revealed a prize they could either bank it, therefore ending their turn or choose to carry on to the next television. If, however, they decided to do that and the next television revealed a 'Hot Spot', all prizes won to that point were lost and play moved to the other team. If the player was lucky then it was possible to make the required number of moves without hitting a 'Hot Spot'. In this case they not only won all the prizes banked up to that point, but

they also carried on playing and got the chance to answer another question.

When the last television monitor was reached, the team decided whether to bank their prizes or answer a final question. A wrong answer meant that prizes not banked to that point were lost and the game continued. A correct answer meant that the team could reach the 'Bonus Game'.

To start, the team bid on how many Hot Spots they were likely to hit. The fewer bid the more money could be won if achieved. The game was now played but choosing top, middle or bottom. A total of thirty monitors hid ten arrows that signified a free move, ten 'Hot Spots' and ten true or false questions. If the team got across to the other side without hitting more 'Hot Spots' than they had initially bid they won various amounts of money. The top prize money was two thousand pounds originally, this was increased to three thousand from series four to ten. The revived Strike it Rich version increased the prize money again to ten thousand pounds.

During the early days of Strike it Lucky there were many highly unusual and eccentric contestants on the show and it became renowned for this. Barrymore would always spend the first five minutes of the show talking to each contestant to reveal just how bonkers some of them were, and this became a hallmark of the show. By 1987, Strike it Lucky had become the fifth most watched programme on British television.

Take Your Pick!

Created by New Zealand television presenter Michael Miles, who also presented the game show initially, Take Your Pick! was a British game show originally broadcast on Radio Luxembourg during the early 1950s. With the launch of ITV, the game show was first broadcast in 1955 and was produced on that channel until 1968, with Michael Miles at the helm throughout. Take Your Pick! was the very first commercial game show televised in the United Kingdom. Although the BBC were also broadcasting game shows at the time, they did not offer cash prizes, whereas Take Your Pick! did and was therefore also the first in the history of British television to do this too.

With the props of a gong (gonged by Alec Dane), an electronic organ (played by Harold Smart) and the voice of English radio and newsreel announcer Bob Danvers-Walker as the game show's announcer, Take Your Pick! contestants had to first get through the 'Yes-No' part of the show. Funnily enough, for this first round the contestants had to answer a series of questions without using the words yes or no or they would be gonged off the stage! The host asked a series of questions for sixty seconds and not only could the contestant not say yes or no, they were not allowed to nod or shake their heads if they wanted to stay in the game show. Modest amounts of money could be won if questions were answered correctly, which led to the height of the show during which the contestants had to make the choice between taking the money or opening the box. The decision was always a gamble because the box could contain some good prizes, a washing

machine or a holiday for example. But it could also contain booby prizes such as a bag of sweets, a mousetrap, breakfast cereals and rotten tomatoes for example.

The final round consisted of boxes numbered one to ten, plus an extra box numbered thirteen. Three boxes contained booby prizes, one contained the star prize (a holiday or small car for example) and the remaining six contained a selection of other prizes. One of these was earmarked as the 'treasure chest' and that box would contain a cash prize and one box included the option to open

box number thirteen. At this stage in the game show Michael Miles would give the contestant a choice between choosing to take up to about fifty pounds in cash or picking a box to open.

The selection of smaller 'other' prizes included things like cowboy hats, pork pies or cinema tickets. The larger prizes would include items such as double beds, sofas, and televisions.

In 1992 Take Your Pick! was revived and ran until 1998. For this new version of the game show, English comedian and singer Des O'Connor was the host.

The Adventure Game

Created by English television producer Patrick Dowling, The Adventure Game was originally a game show aimed at the younger generation, but it ended up becoming very popular with adult audiences too. The first episode was broadcast in 1980 on the BBC and after four series and twenty-two episodes the game show came to an end in 1986. The Adventure Game is credited with being the forerunner to the extremely popular game show The Crystal Maze that was produced some years later.

The concept for The Adventure Game originated because Dowling had an interest in the fantasy table top role-playing game of Dungeons and Dragons and he wanted to bring the same sci-fi feel of the game to television screens. Dowling created just that. The premise for each episode of the game show was that the contestant, accompanied by two celebrity contestants, had all travelled to the planet Arg by spaceship. The tasks the contestants had to carry out to be successful varied with each series - finding a crystal to fuel their spaceship to return back to Earth for example.

Anagrams of the word 'dragon', the planet Arg was inhabited by shape shifting dragons called Argonds. The look, feel and characteristics of the Argonds changed with each series. The other characters that appeared throughout or just in certain series' included The Rangdo, the ruler of planet Arg. In the first series this ruler was in human form and was played by Ian Messiter, the old professor who lived in his velvet jacket. In the second and third series the human form was changed to a somewhat absurd aspidistra that sat on top of a plant stand. When angry it would roar and shake! In the fourth series the Rangdo turned into a teapot that spouted steam when angry. The contestants, when faced with the wrath of the Rangdo, had to placate him quickly by saying 'Gronda! Gronda!' accompanied with a bow or curtsey. Other notable characters included Darong (played by newsreader Moira Stuart), the half-deaf ancient butler Gandor (played Chris Leaver). Gandor accompanied the contestants through the tasks and puzzles and would also referee the Vortex and Drogna games.

The contestants had to complete a number of tasks, games and puzzles to achieve their overall goal and many of these tasks involved a plastic disc called the drogna. This was the currency on the planet Arg. Different coloured drognas had different numbers of sides and were therefore worth different units. There were several tasks that appeared regularly including The Drogna Game. Usually played in the middle of the programme, contestant versus the Red Salamander of Zardil, the contestant had to try and get to the edge of the game board carrying the crystal. This part of the show became so popular that Acornsoft released a version for the BBC Micro computer.

The Vortex was the final task of the show that enabled the contestants to get back to their spaceship. This involved each in turn having to jump between a grid of points whilst facing the opposition known as the Vortex. In series two this was a video-effect-generated pulsing column, and in series three and four a computer-generated flashing column. If the contestant failed and jumped into the Vortex, they would be 'evaporated', lost the game and would have to walk back to Earth along the interplanetary highway. It all seems a little absurd looking back on it, but at the time this was a highly popular and addictive game show for both children and adults alike.

The Crystal Maze

Created by French producer Jacques Antoine, The Crystal Maze was first broadcast on Channel 4 in 1990. The adventure game show ran for six series, totalling eighty-three episodes and finally came to an end in the summer of 1995. One series per year was broadcast and each show lasted for an hour.

The game show consisted of The Crystal Maze set that was made up of four different zones, each of which represented a different period in time and space. Each programme had a team of six contestants all trying to collect as many 'crystals' as they could throughout the different challenges and tasks set. Crystals were worth five second of time, which was then used when they got to the final challenge that took place in the 'Crystal Dome'. The more time the team had accrued throughout the other challenges by winning time crystals,

the more chance of success they had when they got to the final Crystal Dome challenge. Here the team had to grab flying tokens, the gold ones, and put them in a clear box. To win, the team had to collect at least one hundred gold tokens more than silver ones.

The four zones of the Crystal Maze were called Aztec (a sandy village), Futuristic (a space station setting), Medieval (a castle where the host purportedly lived) and Industrial (a modern day chemical plant). The last was replaced by Ocean (a shipwreck scene) from series four onwards. The entire set was not in fact a maze, but these four zones each linked together. At the centre of the four zones stood an enormous geometric acrylic glass dome, the Crystal Dome.

As well as having challenges set in each of the zones, there were also interesting ways of the teams getting from one zone to another. Often this involved climbing net ladders in Ocean, rowing canoes in Aztec, answering the computer's questions in Futuristic and climbing through a gap to get into Industrial.

There were four types of games: skill games, physical games, mental games and mystery games. The team captain would choose who was to play each game and which type, with the aim of that person having the best chance of winning as many time crystals as possible, given their skill set. Each game also had the hazard of a player potentially getting 'locked in' a game room. This could happen if the time limit was exceeded before the contestant got out of the game room. Some games also had automatic lock-ins, which occurred if the player committed a foul.

Between 1990 and 1993 The Crystal Maze was famously presented by New Zealand writer, actor, television presenter and theatre performer Richard O'Brien. For the final two years of the game show this role was then taken over by English musician, singer and actor Edward Tudor-Pole. Both of these presenters had a certain craziness about them, without which arguably the characteristics of the

show, for which is was so popular, would have been somewhat lacking.

The set for the Crystal Maze was, for its time, something extremely impressive and high-tech. It was the size of two football pitches and cost two hundred and fifty thousand pounds to build. The game show's popularity is reflected in the viewing figures and at the height of its popularity between four and six million viewers tuned in. It was also voted as the 'greatest UK game show of all time' in 2006 and 2010.

The Generation Game

British game show The Generation Game was first broadcast in 1971 under the title Bruce Forsyth's Generation Game. It was produced under this guise until 1982. The family friendly game show then returned to our screens in 1990 and ran for a further twelve years. In total twenty-four series and three hundred and seventy-one episodes were broadcast, including forty-six specials.

The time in broadcasting history when The Generation Game was produced was a time when game shows were taking over from variety performance-type shows. Game shows were becoming more popular and were also cheaper to produce. They did not require an expensive theatre to be hired, large numbers of musicians or long rehearsal times, all of which had to be paid for.

The show consisted of eight contestants playing in pairs and they were usually members of the same family. For the first two rounds there were two games in which two pairs competed against each other. A typical type of game at this stage would be the pairs watching a skilled professional do or make something and then the contestants would have a certain amount of time to copy what they had seen. Once the task had been completed (or in some cases not!) the professional would look at each contestant's attempt and result and mark them. This first part of the game show is highly memorable and tasks like sausage making, making a pot on a pottery wheel, ballroom dancing and flower arranging are just some examples that spring to mind. After this the contestants had to compete in a more quiz-based round, which would involve having to do something like identify a

piece of music.

The first section of the show was then repeated with the two other pairs of contestants and the two highest scoring pair went through to the final. The final pairs competed in the same way but this task usually involved a longer set piece that they had to emulate – a musical or dance routine performance for example. The winning couple after this then went through to the final and famous conveyor belt game. An array of prizes would go past the pair on a conveyor belt, after which they had to recall as many as they could. They would then win all the prizes they could remember. Who doesn't remember the cuddly toy, the teas maid and the clock radio?!

During the 1970s The Generation Game became one of the most popular shows on British television and was most definitely one of the BBC's strongest for their Saturday night television line-up.

Bruce Forsyth famously hosted The Generation Game from its start to 1977 initially. He then returned to present the show from 1990 to 1994 and then occasionally in 2007. The show reached its peak viewing figures under Larry Grayson, who hosted the show from 1978 to 1982, when an estimated twenty-five million viewers were watching it. Jim Davidson then took over the reigns from 1995 to 2002.

The Golden Shot

Broadcast in 1967 until 1975, The Golden Shot was a British game show produced for ITV. Each show lasted for an hour and although it had several presenters over the years, English entertainer Bob Monkhouse was arguably the host that is most commonly associated with the show.

Canadian singer, songwriter and television performer Jackie Rae was The Golden Shot's first host. He was then followed by Bob Monkhouse who hosted the programme twice: from 1967 to 1972 and then again from 1974 to 1975. Television and theatre comedian Norman Vaughan then took the helm from 1972 to 1973, followed by ex-footballer and Britain's first well-known mixed race stand-up comedian, Charlie Williams. When Monkhouse returned to the show in 1974 he was joined by co-hostess Wei Wei Wong who had been a part of the Dougie Squires' Second Generation dance troupe. In television production history, this was one of the earliest ever appearances of an Asian woman on British television.

The concept of The Golden Shot involved a crossbow that was attached to a television camera. The crossbow would be shot at an exploding target that had been embedded in an apple. This was positioned on a topical backdrop, famously during the Monkhouse era this was an enlarged cartoon drawn by him. The early programmes of the game show required a contestant to give instructions to blindfolded cameraman Derek Chason to guide him to the correct aim. The contestant would have either been in the studio in an isolation booth, or at home playing over the phone. The contestant would give Chason instructions, left a bit, right a bit, up a bit, down a bit etc. until they said FIRE! In the later years of the game show the game changed so that the contestants actually aimed and fired the crossbow themselves.

To win a sizeable prize the earlier episodes required the contestant to get seven rounds of shots on target. Later on this was reduced to only having to hit four rounds on the target.

In Bob Monkhouse's' autobiography, he related several specific stories from his time hosting the game show. One contestant was playing from a telephone box whilst watching a television from across the road in a rental shop. It would have been fine, apart from when someone in the shop decided to change the channel so the contestant couldn't see what they were aiming at any more! Another story involved a priest who was apparently audibly praying during the show that he wouldn't get hurt by the shooting bolt. Monkhouse recalled how the bolt actually ricocheted off the target only to land right next to the praying priest!

The Krypton Factor

Produced by Granada for ITV and created by Jeremy Fox, The Krypton Factor was a British game show that originally ran from 1977 to 1995. This original show ran for twenty series and totally two hundred and seventy-four episodes. In addition to this, there was also two series of Young Krypton Factor that comprised twenty-one episodes and the adult version was revived briefly between 2009 and 2010.

The Krypton Factor was renowned for being one of the toughest game shows to succeed in. A bit like Mastermind, it had that reputation and aurora about it that earned the contestants willing to take part that of superhuman powers if they successfully completed the difficult challenges set. It is no coincidence that the show's title, The Krypton Factor, was a reference to Superman's home planet Krypton.

Presented by British journalist and broadcaster Gordon Burns for the entire duration of the game show, contestants from all over the United Kingdom and Ireland lined up to compete in games that tested both their mental ability and physical strength and stamina. Each contestant was assigned a colour for the contest, red, green, yellow or blue. The way the show was scored was not referred to just as points, but as their particular 'Krypton Factor', for example, 'the winner, with a Krypton Factor of x is …'

The Krypton Factor rounds consisted of five originally and a sixth (Response) was later added. The contestants could win up to ten points in each round, with the remaining contestants winning less points as their place in the round decreased.

The Personality round required each

contestant to perform a task such as re-writing a nursery rhyme as if it was a news story. The Mental Agility round replaced this after the first series and often took the form of some kind of memory test or having the ability to compute numbers, or remember a sequence of numbers, colours or images for example. They would then be asked a series of progressively hard questions about it.

The Response round changed over different series but was basically a test of aptitude and dexterity. The later 1986 and 1987 series actually used a flight simulator for this round with each contestant being marked by a flight instructor. Over the years the contestants were required to fly various craft including a Harrier Jump Jet, a Sea King helicopter, Concorde, a Hercules and participate in a simulated Red Arrows display.

The Observation round was just as its title suggests. Contestants would typically be shown a specially made video clip or section from an ITV drama series. They would then be asked questions about it in turn or later had to spot the difference. The Physical Ability round was probably the most memorable from the game show and watching contestants try and complete an army assault course was always fascinating and sometimes hilarious! The final two rounds were the Intelligence and the General Knowledge rounds. The Intelligence round usually comprised a two or three-dimensional puzzle where shapes had to be put together to fit in a certain space or make a certain shape. These were memorably both extremely testing and frustrating to watch. The General Knowledge round was a quick-fire question round.

The Price is Right

Created by American television game show producer Bob Stewart, The Price is Right was a British television game show that originally ran on and off during the 1980s, 1990s and into the first decade of this century.

Comedian, actor and game show host Leslie Crowther presented the original version of The Price is Right. English Television presenter Bob Warman presented it the second time round followed by Bruce Forsyth and finally comedian and actor Joe Pasquale.

The contestants for each show were plucked randomly from the audience and they took their places in Contestants Row accompanied by the famous catchphrase 'Come on down!' An object was then shown to them and they each had to guess in turn how much they thought the object was worth. The player who got the closest to the right price joined the host to play a pricing game. This was different every time, but basically involved the contestant having to guess the prices of more objects shown to them. Whether they were good at it or not, the contestant was put through to the next round. After that, another audience member would be picked to join the remaining contestants and the whole process would start again. In the original series' this was repeated six times. It was reduced to three when the game show running time was cut to thirty minutes.

In the original Crowther version of The Price is Right, the six players went to the Supermarket where they had to pick items that added up to a particular total. They then had to spin a numbered wheel trying to get it to stop at number one hundred. The wheel was later removed from the game because of the lack of skill required to win. This was replaced by a quiz on how much things cost, called Check the Difference, with those furthest away from the actual price eliminated each time.

Two contestants survived the above and went on to compete in the Showcase. They again had to estimate the total value of a big stack of prizes and the contestant who got the nearest to the actual total won the entire lot. The spinning wheel did return for the 1990s version of the show and only one contestant went through to the final round. They had to then estimate the value of the showcase and would win it if they got within a specific range of the value. The Bruce Forsyth version had the player pressing a button that stopped on a figure that ranged between a thousand and five thousand pounds. If their guess didn't go over it and was within that amount of the actual, then they won the entire showcase, which could be worth fifteen to twenty-five thousand pounds. The prizes in Bruce's era were at their maximum. With Pasquale's era on the game show the prize price range was significantly reduced to between five hundred and four thousand pounds; a reflection on the country's economic situation.

The Pyramid Game

Created by American television game show producer Bob Stewart, The British game show The Pyramid Game was based on the American version of the show with the same name. It was first broadcast on ITV from 1981 to 1984 and then from 1989 to 1990. The English DJ, television presenter and voiceover artist Steve Jones presented both runs of the show and was renowned for his very large colourful spectacles. In total The Pyramid Game ran for six series and totalled one hundred and fifty-six episodes.

The game show consisted of two contestants who were paired with two celebrities who would, in teams, attempt to beat each other. A bank of six screens structured in a pyramid shape was in the middle of the studio and a title would be showing on each one. These would usually have been cryptic clues to the topic of conversation, some with a certain amount of humour or wit attached to them.

The first round began by a celebrity picking a title from which a subject would be revealed. With thirty seconds to do it, the celebrity then had to describe seven words connected to the subject that the contestant had to guess. They could use any words or gestures they liked as long as they didn't sound like the word in question. If this happened the judges would 'honk' them and they would have to move on to the next word. Every correct answer scored one point. The second celebrity/contestant pair then did the same. This would then be repeated but with each contestant describing the words to the celebrity.

Behind one of the subjects was a

'Lucky 7' symbol for each show. This also had its own identifiable sound motif attached to it. Also, if all seven answers were given within the time a bonus prize was given. This was originally a Pyramid clock, but later on in the series this became a random prize such as a weekend break or a television.

Whichever team scored the highest after these rounds went through to the Winner's Circle. This time the celebrity had to describe actual subjects that the contestant had to guess and they only had sixty seconds in which to describe as many as they could. An example of this would be the subject of 'Chemical Elements' and the words oxygen, hydrogen etc. could be said as a clue to the answer. They could spend as much of the sixty seconds as they liked on one, or they could pass. Miming was not allowed in this round, however, and players would get 'honked' if this or an inappropriate clue was given. The first three answers were worth twenty-five pounds, followed by two at fifty pounds and the final one at one hundred pounds. Guess what? After the adverts this entire process was repeated with the contestants swapping over with the celebrities to do the describing.

The Weakest Link

The game show The Weakest Link was first broadcast in the United Kingdom in 2000 and it ran until 2012. Journalist and television presenter Anne Robinson (famous for her assertive views) hosted the show for the entirety of its run.

The format of the game show consisted of a team of contestants who all had to answer general knowledge questions in turn. Unlike many other game shows, this was a team effort, so points were not won individually but they were won as a team total. The object of each round was to answer consecutively correct answers, therefore creating a chain of which the value of money increased as the chain of correct answers got longer. The money accrued with each correct answer, but if a contestant got an answer wrong and therefore broke the chain, the amount won to that point went straight back to zero. The idea therefore was for contestants to say 'bank' at various points in a sequence of questions as long as it was said just before a question was asked. Once this was said, the money won to that point was then safe and saved. The balance returned to zero, however, every time a contestant said 'bank'. Also money not banked before the clock ran out was also lost. It was perhaps surprising how many times one found themselves screaming 'bank' at the television screen when for some unfathomable reason the clock would be about to get to zero and the team playing seemed totally unaware of the fact that they were about to lose every penny that they had just built up!

At the end of each round the contestants voted for who should be eliminated from the game. They all wrote

who they voted for and then the person with the most votes would be the weakest link and sent packing. Arguably the most remembered and still widely used phrases from the game show, which has certainly crept into modern culture, was the famous Anne Robinson line, 'You are the weakest link, goodbye'. Robinson was also renowned for being pretty gruelling and sarcastic to contestants during the show but particularly once they had been voted as the weakest link.

Obviously, as more contestants got voted off the shorter the rounds became. The following round was also always started with the person who had been voted as the strongest link in the previous round.

The final two rounds consisted of the final two contestants first working together in the same way as the earlier rounds, except this time the money banked at the end was doubled or tripled. The final was then a head-to-head where the two players had to each answer five questions. Whoever answered the most correctly won that day's show outright. In the event of a tie the game finished with Sudden Death.

The Weakest Link format has been successfully licensed all over the world and many countries have their own version. The original British version of the game show is also still broadcast around the world on the BBC Entertainment channel.

Wheel of Fortune

Created by American television host, musician, actor and media mogul Merv Griffin, Wheel of Fortune was a British television game show first broadcast on ITV in 1988. After fourteen series and seven hundred and thirty-seven episodes the show finally came to an end in 2001. The name of the game show reflected the enormous carnival wheel that the contestants got great satisfaction from spinning throughout each episode.

Wheel of Fortune was basically a word game (a bit like hangman). There was a wall with boxes and the numbers of boxes that were lit up indicated the length of the words in the phrase in question. A clue was given for the phrase to be guessed.

The contestants then took it in turns to spin the wheel. This generated a random number of points, guessing a consonant that may have been in the word puzzle and earning them the spun sum of points for every appearance that their chosen consonant appeared in the phrase. They kept spinning the wheel until they landed on 'Lose a Turn' or 'Bankrupt', both of which meant that all points for that round were lost. Points were also lost if they picked a letter that didn't appear in the puzzle. If a player required a vowel to be revealed then they would have to part with points rather than earn them. Because spinning earned points, very often the puzzle would be glaringly obvious, but the contestant wouldn't guess it, they would keep spinning instead, whilst viewers at home were undoubtedly screaming the answer at their television screens in frustration!

The whole point of the spinning was to accrue points but also to guess the answer to the phrase. If guessed correctly, the contestant would end the round and win a prize. This entire process was repeated four times with the last round eliminating the spinning with the highest scorer being given the chance to solve a puzzle with just six chosen letters that was made up of five consonants and a vowel. The jackpot prize was won if this puzzle was answered correctly.

Scottish radio and television presenter and journalist Nicky Campbell originally presented Wheel of Fortune from 1988 to 1996. Most people probably associate their memories of the game show with him in fact. His easy-going gentle nature certainly helped with the show's viewing figures and rating. Former professional footballer, entertainer and actor Bradley Walsh then took over for the 1997 season. Between 1998 and 2001 Scottish television presenter John Leslie hosted the show. Paul Hendy was then the last host of the game show before it came to an end. The role of the letter turner in the show also gained some sort of early television celebrity status. In particular Carol Smillie can thank Wheel of Fortune for helping launch her career as she became just as popular as Nicky Campbell on the show.

Famous catchphrases from the game show included 'We'll see you in the spin

of a wheel', 'One spin of this wheel could mean a possible fortune!' and at the end of the show, 'We'll see you next time around!'

Who Wants to Be a Millionaire?

British television game and quiz show Who Wants to Be a Millionaire? was created by David Briggs, Steve Knight and Mike Whitehill. It was first broadcast on ITV in 1998 and the final episode was aired very recently, in February 2014. In total thirty series were produced totalling five hundred and ninety-two episodes. The game show was presented by British radio and television broadcaster Chris Tarrant OBE.

Originally Who Wants to Be a Millionaire? was broadcast every evening for ten days at a time. It was later moved to the primetime ITV slot on Saturday evenings and it always lasted for an hour. The very first contestant on the show was Graham Elwell and he won sixty-four thousand pounds.

The contestants were members of the public who had applied to the show and although they were chosen randomly, they were also assessed with regard to their ability to answer general knowledge questions. Basically, each contestant had to answer question after question and each time one was correct the amount of money won increased in increments starting with question one that was worth one hundred or five hundred pounds to question fifteen or twelve which was worth one million pounds. The former amounts and numbers were used from 1998 to 2007, the latter from then onwards.

Each contestant could choose to leave the game at any point and take away the amount accrued. In the later version, answering the second question correctly guaranteed them one thousand pounds whatever happened. The contestant also had three lifelines that they could use

once each in order to help them. These were, 'Ask the Audience', 'Fifty/Fifty' where the computer eliminates two wrong answers out of the possible four given, and 'Phone-a-Friend'.

Famous Chris Tarrant catchphrases from the game show include 'But we don't want to give you that', which actually meant that he was joking and wanted the contestant to continue to try and win even more money and 'Is that your final answer?', probably now quoted in every household in Britain when playing any board game with questions!

At its climax in the United Kingdom, which was in 1999, Who Wants to Be a Millionaire? had some nineteen million viewers tuning in to watch it; that is an astonishing one person in three in the country. In the British Film Institute's 2000 list of the '100 Greatest British Television Programmes', Who Wants to Be a Millionaire? came twenty-third. The success of the show was such that it has unsurprisingly been licensed to countries all over the world.

Winner Takes All

Winner Takes All was a British game show that was created by English broadcaster Geoffrey Wheeler. The show was first broadcast on ITV in 1975 and after fourteen series and two hundred and forty-eight episodes, it finally came to an end in 1988. English comedian Jimmy Tarbuck OBE hosted the show from its inception until 1987, it was then hosted in is final year by its creator, Geoffrey Wheeler. It did have one more appearance on television in 1997 when British actor and comedian Bobby Davro hosted it for one series on digital channel Challenge TV.

The show started with two contestants and each started with fifty points. Multiple choice questions were then asked, each with a possible six answers. Attached to each possible answer was a betting odd: Evens, 2-1, 3-1, 4-1, 5-1, and 10-1. The

contestant could therefore decide how many of their points to play with and bet on. They then selected the odds that corresponded with the answer that they thought was correct. If they answered correctly, then the points the odds were worth were added to their score. If incorrect, then the points were lost.

The contestant who scored the most points went through to the final and the poor loser went home with absolutely nothing in the early shows. In the later series they were lucky enough to be given a Filofax! Two winners of a show's rounds would go through to the final, however, where they played for cash. The maximum that could be won was one thousand pounds. The winner took the money they had won plus the option of returning to the show the following week with a chance of increasing their total

winnings. If, however, they returned and then lost, they would end up with only one hundred pounds at the end of the day. The runner-up in the final did get a consolation prize of … wait for it … one hundred pounds!

Sometimes at the start of Winner Takes All during the Jimmy Tarbuck era, he would enter onto the stage carrying a briefcase that contained one thousand pounds in one-pound notes to show off what the Winner Takes All top prize was.

Wipeout

Wipeout was a British game show created by American television producer, writer and actor Bob Fraser. The show was first broadcast on BBC One in 1994 and ran for a total of nine series, totalling four hundred and ninety-five episodes. Wipeout finally came to an end at the end of 2002. Between 1994 and 1997, British magician and television performer Paul Daniels hosted the show. Comedy writer, comedian and actor Bob Monkhouse OBE then took over and presented the show until its final episode in 2002.

Wipeout was a light-hearted quiz game that had three teams playing. The format for the game was that correct answers would be rewarded by a golden star showing, whereas wrong answers or 'Wipeouts' were shown by a blue and yellow 'W'. Later on when Monkhouse was presenting the show this changed so that green ticks represented correct answers and red Xs represented Wipeouts.

Round one consisted of three boards (two in the Monkhouse version). Ten pounds was awarded for the first correct answer and then ten pounds for every subsequent correct answer, up to question eleven. This round had a 'Hot Spot' prize. The sort of prize this was, was determined by where it was hidden. If behind a correct answer then the prize would be something worthwhile, but if behind a Wipeout, it would be a useless cheap prize such as a lollipop! Any player who won a 'Hot Spot' prize got to keep it, regardless of the outcome of the entire game.

'Wipeout Auction' was the name of the second round. With twelve possible answers showing on a grid, the contestants would be offered a certain subject. Four

of the answers were Wipeouts and the other eight would be correct. The highest scoring contestant at this point in the game would then say how many correct answers they could identify on the grid. They could also pass this opening bid to their opponent. Whoever offered the highest bid on the grid got to choose that many answers. The aim was for them to successfully match the number of correct answers they had bid and they continued to do this until they got one wrong and hit a Wipeout. If this happened, the opposing player only had to get one answer right to take control of the next game.

The bonus round followed, which was known as the 'Monkhouse Minute' in Bob's era. Very much like the game in The Price is Right, the contestants had to choose six answers and then run up and press the button to reveal how many correct ones they had actually selected. They would keep doing this until either the time had run out or they had all six correctly selected. This round would win the contestant a wonderful holiday. When Paul Daniels was in charge, the contestants were told before the round where they could be going. In the Monkhouse era, the winner could choose where they went as long as it was in Europe!

Game Show Quiz: Questions

1. Alan Titchmarsh hosted Ask the Family in 1999, but who was the original host?

2. Which snooker player assisted Jim Davidson on Big Break?

3. Name the three hosts of Blankety Blank?

4. Which quiz had a catchphrase of I'll have a 'P' Bob?

5. Tony Green assisted Jim Bowen on which TV quiz show?

6. Robin Ray, Robert Robinson & Bob Holness have all hosted which panel game?

7. What was the first game show shown on Channel 4?

8. What are the names of the two men who have hosted The Crystal Maze?

9. William G. Stewart hosts which TV quiz show?

10. Friends Like These was hosted by which former pop duo?

11. What were the names of the FOUR original hosts of Game for A Laugh?

12. Who was Larry Grayson's 'Glamorous Assistant' on The Generation Game?

13. Lionel Blair and Una Stubs were the original team captains on which charades based game show?

14. Who are the two team captains on Have I Got News for You?

15. Stuart Hall and Eddie Waring hosted which over the top 'sports' challenge game show?

16. John Hart, Roger Pritchard, Sir David Hunt & Fred Housego have all won which cerebral quiz show?

17. Who hosts the TV quiz It's Only TV But I Like It?

18. Who hosted the cerebral & action quiz The Krypton Factor?

19. Which two people have hosted the BBC's Masterchef?

20. What was the booby prize on 3-2-1

21. True or False, Russ Abbott once hosted "Stars In Their Eyes"?

22. Who originally hosted "Blockbusters"?

23. What decade did we first see the show "Krypton Factor", hosted by Gordon Burns?

24. What was the first programme to be shown on Channel 4?

25. On "Crystal Maze", which of the following has never been an adventure zone: Industrial, Aztec, Desert or Medieval?

26. A record for the shortest quiz run on UK television has to go to "Shafted" which ironically got shafted from our screens after three shows. Who was the host?

27. "Whittle" was a show hosted by Tim Vine for Channel 5 and later Challenge TV. This show was a blatant rip-off of which ITV format?

28. The US show "Cards Sharks" has been shown in the UK since 1980 under what name?

29. Who was the original host of "Family Fortunes"?

30. What year was "Mastermind" first shown on UK television?

31. Name the show that contained the catchphrase, 'All right my love'?

32. First broadcast on the BBC in 1951, which show had a panel that included Gilbert Harding and Lady Isabel Barnett?

33. Who was the original presenter of "Take Your Pick" in 1955?

34. What was the maximum prize in "Double Your Money" from 1955 to 1968?

35. What was the quiz on the children's programme "Crackerjack", where wrong answers were rewarded with cabbages called?

36. Who was the original presenter of "University Challenge"?

37. Who loaded the cross bows in "The Golden Shot"?

38. On which show did Simon Cowell make his TV début?

39. Which show featured Dusty Bin?

40. Combining quiz, puzzle solving and physical challenges, what was the name of the show originally presented by Gordon Burns?

41. What was the name of the quiz show based on Noughts and Crosses?

42. Who was the first "Sky-runner" in "Treasure Hunt"?

43. Bob Monkhouse presented "Family Fortunes" from 1980-83 and Les Dennis presented from 1987-2002. Who was the presenter between 1983 and 1985?

44. In which Channel 4 show did contestants choose "Question or Nominate"?

45. Who were the THREE presenters of "Blankety-Blank"?

46. Who were the team captains on "Give Us a Clue"?

47. Who was the original presenter of "A Question of Sport" on national TV?

48. And who were the original team captains?

49. How many letters are there in the "Countdown" conundrum?

50. Who presented "Catchphrase" from 1986 to 1999?

Game Show Quiz: Answers

1. Robert Robinson

2. John Virgo

3. Terry Wogan, Les Dawson and Lily Savage

4. Blockbusters

5. Bullseye

6. Call My Bluff

7. Countdown (Also the first programme shown on channel 4)

8. Richard O'Brien and Edward Tudor Pole

9. Fifteen To One

10. Ant and Dec (Ant McPartlin and Decland Donnelly)

11. Jeremy Beadle, Matthew Kelly, Henry Kelly, Sarah Kennedy

12. Isla St Clair

13. Give Us A Clue

14. Paul Merton and Ian Hislop

15. It's A Knockout

16. Mastermind

17. Jonathan Ross

18. Gordon Burns

19. Lloyd Grossman & Gary Rhodes

20. Dusty Bin

21. True. Russ Abbott hosted a one-off Elvis special

22. Bob Holness

23. 1970s – 1977 to be precise

24. Countdown

25. Desert Zone

26. Robert Kilroy-Silk

27. Everybody's Equal

28. Play Your Cards Right

29. Bob Monkhouse

30. 1972

31. The Generation Game, spoken by Bruce Forsyth

32. What's My Line

33. Michael Miles

34. £1,000

35. Double or Drop

36. Bamber Gascoigne

37. Bernie the Bolt

38. Sale of the Century, as a contestant in 1998

39. 3-2-1

40. The Krypton Factor

41. Criss-Cross Quiz

42. Anneka Rice

43. Max Bygraves

44. Fifteen to One

45. Terry Wogan, Les Dawson and Lily Savage (Paul O'Grady)

46. Lionel Blair and Una Stubbs

47. David Vine (a regional version was presented by Stuart Hall in 1968)

48. Cliff Morgan and Henry Cooper

49. Nine

50. Roy Walker

The pictures in this book were provided courtesy of the following:

WIKICOMMONS
commons.wikimedia.org

Design & Artwork by Scott Giarnese

Published by Demand Media Limited

Publishers: Jason Fenwick & Jules Gammond

Written by Michelle Brachet